healthy and simple
asian recipes

for delicious everyday meals

Asian cooking is not only healthy but flavorful.
This handy book contains over 50 nutritious and delicious
recipes—like Fresh Japanese Tofu Salad with Miso Dressing,
Chinese Chicken Salad and Mapo Tofu.

PERIPLUS EDITIONS
Singapore • Hong Kong • Indonesia

Contents

MAIL ORDER SOURCES

Finding the ingredients for Asian home cooking has become very simple. Most super-markets carry staples such as soy sauce, fresh ginger, and fresh lemongrass. Almost every large metropolitan area has Asian markets serving the local population—just check your local business directory. With the Internet, exotic Asian ingredients and cooking utensils can be easily found online. The following list is a good starting point of online merchants offering a wide variety of goods and services.

http://www.asiafoods.com
http://www.geocities.com/MadisonAvenue/8074/VarorE.html
http://dmoz.org/Shopping/Food/Ethnic_and_Regional/Asian/
http://templeofthai.com/
http://www.orientalpantry.com/
http://www.zestyfoods.com/
http://www.thaigrocer.com/Merchant/index.htm
http://asianwok.com/
http://pilipinomart.com/
http://www.indiangrocerynet.com/
http://www.orientalfoodexpress.com/

Who hasn't benefited from a bowl of chicken soup when they've been sick with a cold or flu? That warm and soothing bowl of soup is more than just comfort food. Chicken soup does help clear nasal clog. Not only do the vapors from the hot liquid clear stuffy nasal passages, but the onions and garlic used in the soup also have antiseptic qualities.

People have known about the health-promoting and healing qualities of various foods almost as long as there have been people, but Asian cooks have made an art of cooking for health. Indeed, much of what you see on the shelves in Asian food shops is also available in herbal remedies from the Chinese doctor around the corner.

This book is a collection of recipes that not only taste fabulous, but can help you and your family maintain optimum health. Many of the ingredients in these recipes are more than just nutritious—from the everyday onion and garlic to Chinese red dates and ginseng, they have actual medicinal value. In addition to having loads of vitamin C, the dates are said to improve blood quality and cure insomnia. Ginseng has so many healing properties that part of its scientific name is panax, as in panacea. This general tonic is used for nearly everything from enhancing athletic performance to soothing motion sickness.

The tiger lily buds, bamboo pith and wolfberries in the wonderful Cooling Clear Soup are said to calm "liver fire" and thus relax the nervous system. Ginger, used often in the West to settle stomachs, has a long list of benefits, reportedly including curing chills in elephants! And that protein-rich culinary chameleon tofu has no cholesterol and minimal saturated fats, but heaps of isoflavones and phytoestrogens.

So experiment with some of these exotic but easy-to-find ingredients. You'll be surprised how tasty keeping healthy can be.

Basic Asian Ingredients

Bamboo shoots are the fresh shoots of the bamboo plant. Pre-cooked bamboo shoots, packed in water, can be found in the refrigerated section of supermarkets. Canned bamboo shoots are also pre-cooked but should be boiled for 5 minutes to refresh before using.

Black bean paste is made from fermented black or yellow soybeans, and is an important seasoning in Asian dishes. **Black bean paste (*tau cheo*)** has a strong, salty flavor, while **yellow bean paste (*miso*)** is slightly sweet. "Sweet" and "hot" salted beans have added sugar or garlic and chili. Soybean pastes are available at Asian food stores.

Black Chinese mushrooms, also known as shiitake mushrooms, are used widely in Asian cooking. The dried ones must be soaked in hot water to soften before use, from 15 minutes to an hour, depending on the thickness. The stems are removed and discarded; only the caps are used. Fresh shiitake mushroom stems can be eaten if the bottoms are trimmed. Substitute porcini mushrooms. Fresh shiitake are increasingly available in supermarkets.

Chili peppers come in many shapes, sizes and colors. Fresh green and red Asian **finger-length chilies** are moderately hot. Tiny red, green or orange **bird's-eye chilies** (*chili padi*) are very hot. **Dried chilies** are usually deseeded, cut into lengths and soaked in warm water to soften before use. **Chili oil** is made from dried chilies or chili powder infused in oil, which is used to enliven some Sichuan dishes.

Thai basil *(horapa)*

Lemon basil *(manglak)*

Basil is used as a seasoning and garnish in many Asian cuisines. Two varieties are used in this book. **Thai basil (*horapa*)** tastes rather like Italian sweet basil but with an added hint of anise, and is used in red and green curries as well as salads and stir-fries. It is available year round. If you cannot find it, use Italian basil. **Lemon basil (*manglak*)** has a lemony flavor that goes well with soups and salads. Basil doesn't store well, so buy it just before you intend to use it.

Chinese cabbage, also known as Napa cabbage, has crinkled, very pale green leaves at the end of long, wide, white-ribbed stalks. Chinese cabbage is pleasantly crisp when raw, and has a slightly sweet flavor which intensifies after long, slow cooking.

Japanese *sansho* pepper is made from the ground seeds of the Japanese prickly ash plant. Available in small glass bottles in Asian food stores, it gives a hot flavor to fatty foods such as eel. Substitute dried Sichuan pepper or ground red cayenne pepper.

Coriander is an indispensable herb and spice in Asian cooking. **Coriander seeds** are roasted and then ground in spice pastes. **Coriander roots** are used in the same way, while **coriander leaves** (also known as cilantro or Chinese parsley) are used as an herb and a garnish.

Fish sauce is made from salted, fermented fish or shrimp. Good quality fish sauce is golden-brown in color and has a salty tang. It is available in bottles in most supermarkets.

Galangal is similar in appearance to ginger and a member of the same family. This aromatic root has a distinctive flavor that is used in dishes throughout Asia. Dried galangal lacks the fragrance of fresh galangal, so try to buy it fresh. It can be sliced and kept sealed in the freezer for several months.

Kaffir lime leaves are used as an herb in soups and curries of Thai, Malay or Indonesian origin. They are also thinly sliced and used as a garnish. Buy them fresh, frozen or dried—fresh or frozen leaves are more fragrant.

Daikon radish is a large, crisp, white-fleshed tuber similar to a carrot, with a sweet and clean flavor. It can be eaten raw, or cooked as a vegetable. The skin needs to be peeled or scrubbed before using. Daikon is available from Asian markets and many well-stocked supermarkets.

Dashi soup stock powder is used to make dashi fish stock and as a basic seasoning in many soups and salad dressings. Substitute another soup stock powder or bouillon cubes if unavailable.

Japanese rice is a short grain variety that is slightly more starchy than Thai or Chinese long grain rice. Available from most supermarkets, you may substitute any other short or medium grain rice.

Mirin is a type of sweetened rice wine sold in bottles in Japanese stores. It is used only for cooking—the alcohol dissipates during cooking. Add $1/_2$ teaspoon sugar to 2 teaspoons sake as a substitute for 1 tablespoon mirin.

Miso is a salty paste made from fermented soy beans. It has a distinctive aroma and flavor, and is an important ingredient in Japanese cuisine. Miso is sold in plastic packs or tubs in the refrigerated section of Asian food stores. Chinese yellow bean paste is similar and may be used as a substitute.

Nori seaweed, also referred to as laver, is toasted, crisp and sold in very thin dark green sheets of varying sizes—these sheets are used for wrapping sushi. Before using, hold a *nori* sheet over an open flame for a few seconds so that it becomes lightly toasted, or toast it in the oven.

Nori is also available as thinly shredded strips or flakes, both of which are used as a garnish served with rice.

Oyster sauce is the rich, thick and dark extract of dried oysters. It is frequently added to stir-fried vegetable and meat dishes, and must be refrigerated once the bottle is opened. Expensive versions made with abalone and vegetarian versions made from mushrooms are also available. Check the ingredients

Fresh yellow wheat noodles (*mee*)

Dried rice vermicelli (*beehoon* or *mifen*)

Dried bean thread noodles (*tang hoon*)

Flat rice noodles (*kway teow*)

Buckwheat noodles (*soba*)

Noodles are a universal favorite in Asia. Both fresh and dried noodles are made from either wheat, rice or bean flour. **Fresh yellow wheat noodles** are thick, spaghetti-like noodles made from wheat flour and egg. Substitute fresh spaghetti or fettucine if you cannot find them. **Dried rice vermicelli (*beehoon* or *mifen*)** are very fine rice threads that must be plunged into hot water to soften before use. **Rice stick noodles** (also known as "river noodles", *kway teow* or *hofun*) are wide, flat rice noodles sold fresh in Asian markets. If not available, use **dried rice stick noodles** instead. **Soba noodles** are slender Japanese noodles made from buckwheat. **Dried bean thread noodles** (*tang hoon*) are dried translucent noodles made from mung bean starch, which are reconstituted by pouring hot water over them.

listed on the bottle as many brands are loaded with MSG.

Rice wine is frequently used in Asian cooking. Japanese sake, mirin or a dry sherry may all be used as substitutes.

Sake or rice wine is available in many different grades. Besides being popular as a drink, sake is an important ingredient in Japanese cooking. Widely available in liquor stores or in supermarkets, it is also sold in the form of cooking sake in Asian supermarkets. Keep refrigerated after opening. Chinese rice wine or dry sherry may be substituted.

Sea salt is available in fine or coarse crystals and is recommended for pickling and preserving. It is slightly milder in taste and imparts a purer flavor to foods.

used for marinades, sauces and soups, or as a table condiment. Its nutty, smoky flavor has become a hallmark of north Asian cuisine.

Sesame seeds are available in black and white varieties, although white seeds are more common. **Sesame paste** is made from ground, roasted sesame seeds and comes covered with oil in glass jars. It is quite hard and needs to be mixed with a little sesame oil or water to make it into a smooth paste. If you cannot find it, use Middle Eastern tahini mixed with some sesame oil to give it a more pronounced flavor.

Shiso leaves (also known as perilla leaves) have an attractive dark green color, sometimes with reddish veins, and are widely used in Japanese cooking either as an ingredient or a garnish. It is a member of the mint family, and the leaves have a hint of basil and spearmint.

Sichuan peppercorns are not really pepper, but a round, reddish-brown berry with a pronounced fragrance and acidic flavor. Also known as Chinese

Sesame oil is extracted from sesame seeds that have been toasted, producing a dark, dense and highly aromatic oil that can be

Dark soy sauce   Light soy sauce

Soy sauce is a fermented sauce brewed from soybeans, water, wheat and salt. **Regular** or **light soy sauce** is very salty and used as a table dip and cooking seasoning. **Dark soy sauce** is thicker and less salty and adds a smoky flavor to dishes.

| Firm tofu | Pressed tofu (*tau kwa*) | Soft tofu |

Tofu or beancurd comes in various forms. **Soft tofu** is silky and smooth but difficult to cook because it falls apart. **Firm tofu** holds its shape well when cut or cooked and has a stronger, slightly sour taste. **Pressed tofu** (often confusingly labeled as firm tofu) is a type of firm tofu that has had much of the water pressed out of it and is therefore much firmer in texture and excellent for stir-fries. Refrigerate fresh tofu, submerged in water, in a plastic container.

pepper or flower pepper (*hua jiao* in Mandarin), it has a sharp pungency that tingles and slightly numbs the lips and tongue, an effect known in Chinese as *ma la* "numb hot." Japanese *sansho* pepper, sold in small bottles, contains other ingredients, but has a similar flavor.

Turmeric root resembles ginger when fresh but is commonly sold in dried form as ground turmeric. It turns dishes bright yellow and has a mild flavor. **Ground turmeric** powder is sold in the spice section of supermarkets.

Vinegar is used in many Asian sauces; unless the recipe calls for a specific variety of vinegar, the best choices are rice vinegar or apple cider vinegar. **Rice vinegar** is mild and faintly fragrant, and is the preferred vinegar throughout Asia. Inexpensive brands from China are readily available in the West. If you cannot obtain rice vinegar, use distilled white vinegar or cider vinegar.

Wasabi paste, a traditional condiment served with Japanese sushi, is made from a root similar to horseradish. Available as a paste or in powdered form to be mixed with water.

Woodear fungus has very little flavor and is added to dishes for its crunchy texture and as a meat substitute. It is sold dried in plastic packets in most Asian supermarkets and comes in small, crinkly sheets. Soak them in water before using, rinse well and discard any hard bits in the center of the larger pieces.

Cucumber Daikon Salad with Sweet Mirin Dressing

2 daikon radishes, peeled and sliced into matchsticks, soaked in cold water for 10 minutes and drained
2 small Japanese cucumbers or English (hothouse) cucumbers shaved into long, flat strips using a peeler, stopping before you reach the seeds
1 small carrot, cut into matchsticks
$^1/_2$ small onion, thinly sliced, soaked in water and drained
2 sheets *nori* seaweed, toasted, halved and sliced thinly (see note)
2 teaspoons black sesame seeds

Sweet Mirin Dressing
2 tablespoons soy sauce
2 tablespoons mirin or sake
1 teaspoon white sugar
2 tablespoons rice vinegar
$^1/_2$ teaspoon *dashi* soup stock powder dissolved in 1 tablespoon water

Before use, hold a *nori* sheet over an open flame for a few seconds so that it becomes lightly toasted, or toast it in a toaster oven.

1 To make the Sweet Mirin Dressing, combine all the ingredients in a small bowl and set aside.

2 To assemble the salad, toss the daikon radish, cucumber or gherkins, carrot and drained onion slices in a medium bowl. Pile the tossed vegetables high on a medium serving plate, pour over the prepared Dressing immediately before serving and top with the toasted *nori* and sesame seeds.

Serves 4–6   Preparation time: 15 mins

Tofu Appetizer

1 cake (10 oz/300 g) firm tofu
1 teaspoon potato starch or cornstarch, for coating
Oil for deep-frying
2 tablespoons grated fresh ginger
2 tablespoons thinly sliced green onions (scallions)
2 tablespoons bonito flakes (see note)
Dark soy sauce, to drizzle over the top

Serves 4
Preparation time: 10 mins
Cooking time: 5 mins

1 Drain the tofu and cut into 4 pieces. Place each piece between 2 clean tea towels and gently place a light weight on top, to squeeze out as much water as possible. Let stand for 5 minutes.

2 Remove the weight from the tofu and dust with the potato or cornstarch, shaking lightly to remove excess.

3 Heat the oil in a skillet or wok over high heat and fry the tofu slices until lightly browned, turning once, then remove from the pan and drain on paper towels. Serve immediately in a small plate topped with the ginger, green onions, bonito flakes and drizzled with soy sauce to taste.

Bonito flakes are shavings of dried, smoked and cured bonito fish, sold in fine or coarse flakes in small plastic packs. Fine flakes are used as a garnish, while coarse flakes are used to make bonito fish stock (*dashi*). Store unused flakes in an airtight container or plastic bag.

Fresh Tofu Salad with Miso Dressing

1 cake (10 oz/300 g) soft tofu
1 tomato, finely diced
1 Japanese or English (hothouse) cucumber, thinly sliced
2 tablespoons finely sliced green onions (scallions)
1 teaspoon miso paste
2 teaspoons sesame oil
2 teaspoons rice vinegar
1 teaspoon sugar
1 teaspoon water
$^1/_2$ cup (25 g) alfalfa sprouts
1 sheet *nori* seaweed, toasted (see note), cut in half, then into thin strips
2 teaspoons sesame seeds, toasted (see note)

1 Drain the tofu and slice in half lengthwise. Cut the halves into $^1/_4$-in (6-mm) thick pieces and lay on a serving plate.

2 In a small bowl gently combine the tomato, cucumber and green onions. Place over the tofu.

3 In another bowl combine the miso paste, sesame oil, rice vinegar, sugar and water to make a dressing. Spoon the dressing over the tofu. Top with the alfalfa sprouts and *nori*. Sprinkle with the sesame seeds.

Before use, hold the *nori* sheet over an open flame for a few seconds so that it becomes lightly toasted, or toast it in a toaster oven.

Toast the sesame seeds in a dry frying pan over medium heat stirring or shaking the pan, until golden brown. Keep moving the seeds so they do not burn.

Serves 4
Preparation time: **10 mins**

Japanese Daikon and Carrot Salad

1³/₄ cups (450 ml) water
1 tablespoon salt
1¹/₂ cups (200 g) daikon radish, peeled and cut into long strips
1 small carrot, peeled and cut into strips
3 tablespoons rice vinegar
1 tablespoon mirin
1 tablespoon soy sauce
1 tablespoon toasted sesame seeds

1 Place 1¹/₂ cups (375 ml) of the water and salt in a medium bowl. Place the daikon radish and carrot in the salted water for 30 minutes, then drain and set aside.
2 Combine the vinegar, remaining water, mirin and soy sauce in a small saucepan and bring to a boil over medium heat. Add the carrot and daikon radish and simmer for 1–2 minutes until tender. Remove from the heat and set aside to cool.
3 Place the carrot and daikon radish between paper towels and squeeze gently to remove any excess vinegar. Place in individual small bowls, sprinkle over the sesame seeds and serve.

Serves 4–6
Preparation time: 5 mins + 30 mins soaking time
Cooking time: 5 mins

Green Beans in Sesame Dressing

1 ³/₄ cups (175 g) fresh or frozen green beans, tops and tails removed, sliced as shown
1 ¹/₂–2 tablespoons sesame paste (see note)
1 teaspoon sugar
2 teaspoons soy sauce
1 tablespoon sake
1 teaspoon rice vinegar
¹/₄ teaspoon *dashi* soup stock powder dissolved in 1 tablespoon water
1 teaspoon miso paste

1 Blanch the green beans in a medium saucepan with 2 cups boiling salted water for 3–5 minutes or until just tender and a bright green color. Immediately plunge into ice cold water until cold, then drain well.
2 Combine the sesame paste, sugar, soy sauce, sake, vinegar, *dashi* and miso paste in a large mixing bowl and toss the beans through the mixture. Serve warm or at room temperature.

Japanese **sesame paste** is made from toasted sesame seeds that are crushed to make a butter. Substitute tahini or freshly ground pan-toasted sesame seeds.

Serves 4
Preparation time: **10 mins**
Cooking time: **5 mins**

Simple Cucumber Salad with Sesame Dressing

1 lb (500 g) baby cucumbers, washed
2 teaspoons salt
2 tablespoons finely chopped garlic,
1–2 small chili peppers, deseeded and sliced (optional)

Sesame Dressing
1 tablespoon sugar
$1/_2$ teaspoon ground Sichuan peppercorn
1 tablespoon vinegar
2 teaspoons sesame oil
$1/_2$ teaspoon ground black pepper

1 Cut each cucumber in half lengthwise, then cut each half into $1^1/_4$ in (3 cm) sections crosswise. Place the cucumbers in a bowl, add the salt, toss to coat the pieces evenly, and let stand for 15 minutes. Rinse the cucumbers in cold water to remove the salt, then drain in a colander.

2 Meanwhile, combine all the Sesame Dressing ingredients in a bowl. Mix well and set aside.

3 Place the drained cucumbers into a serving bowl and add the garlic, chili and Dressing. Stir to blend the flavors. Serve.

Serves 4
Preparation time: 20 mins
Assembling time: 2 mins

Thai Green Papaya Salad

A refreshing and unusual salad made with shredded green papaya, it stands alone or takes such additions as cooked shrimp or beef jerky to turn it into a main dish.

1 large ripe tomato, cut into wedges
1 green papaya (1 lb/ 500 g), peeled and coarsely grated to yield 3 cups
1 carrot, coarsely grated to yield 1 cup
2 tablespoons chopped mint leaves
Sprigs of mint leaves, to garnish

Dressing
3 tablespoons lime juice
3 tablespoons fish sauce
1 tablespoon sugar
2 cloves garlic, minced
1 small chili pepper, deseeded and sliced
2 tablespoons toasted sesame seeds (see note)

Serves 4
Preparation time: **15 mins**

Toast the sesame seeds in a frying pan over medium heat until golden brown. Keep moving the pan so the seeds do not burn.

Combine the Dressing ingredients in a large bowl and mix until the sugar is dissolved, then add all the other ingredients (except sprigs of mint leaves) and toss well to combine. Transfer to a serving platter, garnish with the mint leaves and serve immediately.

Tofu with Sweet Sesame Soy Dressing

8 cups (2 liters) water
1 cake (10 oz/300 g)
  firm tofu
1 tablespoon minced garlic
1 tablespoon minced
  ginger
3 green onions (scallions),
  minced
1 sprig fresh coriander
  leaves (cilantro), minced

Sauce
1 tablespoon sesame oil
1 tablespoon chili oil
1 tablespoon soy sauce
1 teaspoon ground black
  pepper
$1/2$ teaspoon salt
1 teaspoon sugar

1 Bring the water to a boil in a medium pot, carefully add the tofu, reduce the heat and simmer for 4 minutes. Remove with a slotted spoon and drain. Alternatively, place the tofu in a steamer and steam for 4 minutes.

2 Mix all the Sauce ingredients well and set aside.

3 Place the garlic, ginger, green onions and coriander leaves in a bowl. Pour over the Sauce and blend well. Place the tofu in the center of a small serving dish. Make 4 cuts across the top of the tofu in both directions, cutting no more than halfway deep. Drizzle the Sauce mixture evenly over the tofu and serve.

Serves 4
Preparation time: **10 mins**
Cooking time: **5 mins**

Fresh Tuna with Ginger Soy Dressing

2 tablespoons thinly sliced leek
1 baby cucumber, washed
2 fresh shiso or large basil leaves, thinly sliced
1 1/2 teaspoons grated ginger
14 oz (400 g) fresh sashimi-grade tuna
Black sesame seeds (optional)

Ginger Soy Dressing
1 1/2 teaspoons grated ginger
1/2 teaspoon dark soy sauce

1 Place the leeks in a small bowl of cold water and soak for 5 minutes. Drain and pat dry with paper towels. Shred the cucumber into long, thin strips and set aside.
2 Combine the sliced leeks and shredded shiso or basil leaves in a small bowl. Add half of the grated ginger and toss well to combine. Dice the tuna and combine with the leek mixture.
3 To prepare the Ginger Soy Dressing, divide the ginger between 4 small sauce bowls and top with the dark soy sauce to taste.
4 Divide the tuna mixture into 4 equal portions. Place each portion on a serving dish. Sprinkle with the black sesame seeds, if desired. Garnish with the reserved shredded cucumber and serve with the Ginger Soy Dressing on the side.

Serves 4
Preparation time: **12–15 mins**

Fresh Bean Sprout and Carrot Salad

4 cups (200 g) bean
sprouts, tops and tails
removed
2 green onions (scallions),
cut into lengths
1 small carrot, cut into
matchsticks to yield
1 cup

Dressing
$3/_4$ cup (185 ml) white
vinegar
2 tablespoons sugar
1 tablespoon salt
1 cup (250 ml) water

1 Combine all the vegetables in a large bowl and
set aside.
2 In a saucepan, bring the Dressing ingredients to a
boil over medium heat. Reduce the heat and simmer
for 1 to 2 minutes, stirring occasionally, until the sugar
is dissolved. Remove and set aside to cool.
3 Pour the cooled Dressing over the vegetables, mix
well and allow to marinate for at least 1 hour. Drain
before serving.

Serves 4
Preparation time: 10 mins + 1 hour to marinate
Cooking time: 5 mins

Salted Chinese Cabbage Pickles

1 small head Chinese
  cabbage (Napa)
1 tablespoon salt
3 teaspoons sugar
1 small chili pepper,
  deseeded and thinly
  sliced (optional)

Serves 8–10
Preparation time: 5–8 mins
  + overnight standing

1 Remove the core of the cabbage, making sure the cabbage remains in one piece. Wash well, shake to remove excess water and squeeze as much liquid from the cabbage as possible. Pat dry with paper towels. Cut the cabbage into 3-cm sections crosswise.

2 Rub half of the salt, sugar and chili into the sections of the cabbage. Sprinkle a little salt and sugar in the base of a plastic bowl and stand each section of the cabbage upright, side by side. Top with the remaining salt, sugar and chili, if using, and cover with a lid. Place a heavy weight on top to weigh the cabbage down and let stand overnight or for 1 day in a cool place or in the refrigerator.

3 To serve, rinse the cabbage leaves well, cut into bite-sized pieces and arrange on a plate or in a shallow bowl.

Chinese Chicken Salad

2 boneless chicken breasts, cut in half
2 small carrots, cut into thin strips
1 English (hothouse) cucumber, cut into thin strips
2 tablespoons roasted peanuts or sesame seeds, coarsely chopped
2 green onions (scallions), thinly sliced
1 tablespoon chopped fresh coriander leaves (cilantro)
1 small chili pepper, seeds removed and thinly sliced (optional)

Marinade
2 tablespoons ginger juice (see note)
2 tablespoons rice wine
$1/2$ teaspoon salt
1 teaspoon sugar

Dressing
$1/4$ cup (60 ml) chicken stock (from fresh stock or bouillon cubes)
3 tablespoons oyster sauce (see note)
1 teaspoon sugar
$1/4$ teaspoon ground pepper
1 teaspoon sesame oil

1 Combine the Marinade ingredients in a mixing bowl, mix thoroughly then set aside.
2 Add the chicken to the Marinade, toss to coat thoroughly, then set aside to marinate for 1 hour.
3 Drain the chicken and place it in a steamer and steam for 10 minutes. Remove and set aside to cool, then cut or tear the meat into strips.
4 Arrange the carrot and cucumber on a platter and top with the steamed chicken.
5 Put all the Dressing ingredients into a small saucepan and bring to a boil. Spoon the hot Dressing over the chicken. Sprinkle with the chopped peanuts and green onions, coriander leaves and sliced chili, if using, and serve.

To make the **ginger juice,** grate 4 in (10 cm) young ginger to make $1/2$ cup of grated ginger. Mix with 2 tablespoons water, then strain the mixture through a fine sieve, pressing with the back of a spoon, to obtain $1/4$ cup (60 ml) of ginger juice.

Serves 2
Preparation time: **40 mins**
Cooking time: **20 mins**

Tofu and Mushroom Lettuce Cups

1 cake (10 oz/300 g)
  firm tofu, finely diced
¹/₄ teaspoon salt
¹/₂ cup (125 ml) oil
1 teaspoon finely
  chopped shallots
1 teaspoon finely
  chopped garlic
4 tablespoons dried
  shrimp, soaked and finely chopped (see note)
2 sweet dried Chinese
  sausages or *lap cheong*,
  diced (see note)
2 water chestnuts,
  peeled and diced
4 fresh black Chinese
  mushrooms, diced
¹/₄ cup (30 g) diced carrot
¹/₄ cup (40 g) diced bell
  pepper
1 small chili pepper,
  deseeded and chopped
1 teaspoon rice wine
¹/₄ cup (60 ml) chicken
  or vegetable stock
1 tablespoon oyster
  sauce (see note)
1–2 teaspoons soy sauce
1 teaspoon sugar
¹/₄ teaspoon ground
  black pepper
1 teaspoon sesame oil
Several large lettuce
  leaves, torn to make
  serving cups as shown
2 tablespoons chopped
  fresh coriander leaves
  (cilantro), to garnish

1 Sprinkle the diced tofu with the salt.

2 Heat the oil in a wok and deep-fry the tofu until golden brown, 2–3 minutes. Remove the tofu and drain.

3 Discard all but 1 tablespoon of the oil in the wok and stir-fry the shallots and garlic until fragrant, about 1 minute. Stir in the dried shrimp, Chinese sausages, water chestnuts, mushrooms and carrot, then stir-fry for 2 minutes.

4 Add the tofu, bell pepper and chili. Pour in the wine, then add the chicken or vegetable stock and the remaining ingredients. Stir briskly until evenly mixed. Divide among the lettuce leaves and serve garnished with the chopped coriander leaves.

Sweet dried Chinese sausages (*lap cheong*) are perfumed with rose-flavored wine. Generally sold in pairs, these sausages keep without refrigeration and are normally sliced and cooked with other ingredients rather than being eaten on their own. They should not be eaten raw. Substitute any sweet, dried sausage or meat jerky.

Dried shrimp are sold in plastic packets or in bins in Asian markets. Choose dried shrimp that are pink in color and soak them in water to soften before use.

Serves 2–3
Preparation time: 30 mins
Cooking time: 20 mins

Chinese Pickled Vegetables

Pickled cabbage dishes, such as the traditional *kimchees* of Korea, are traditional fare throughout Asia, and even Europe has its versions, like the German *sauerkraut*. Pickled cabbage has a wide range of benefits to human health. It contains live enzymes that facilitate digestion of other foods that are eaten with it and it reduces cholesterol. According to Chinese medicine it tones the spleen and stomach, and the chilies, Sichuan peppercorns and other spices in the Sichuan version drive dampness from the body and protect it from parasites and microbes. This dish may be prepared in large quantities and kept in a covered jar in the refrigerator so that you can serve a small side dish of it with all your main meals.

12 cups (3 liters) water
1 large or 2 small heads of cabbage (not Chinese cabbage), washed and leaves separated (large leaves torn into chunks)
6 slices ginger
1 leek, halved lengthwise, then cut in lengths
2–3 small chili peppers, halved lengthwise then cut into three sections
4 stalks celery, sliced
1 carrot, sliced
1 daikon radish, cut on angle into slices

Seasoning
10 Sichuan peppercorns
3 cups (750 ml) vodka
2 teaspoons sea salt

1 Pour the water into a clean wide-mouthed glass or ceramic vessel that will hold at least 16 cups (4 liters).
2 Add the Seasoning, then the cabbage, then all the remaining ingredients on top of the cabbage. Do not stir. Cover the vessel tightly with a lid (place a weight on top if necessary to keep a tight seal), and set aside to pickle for 3 days.
3 After 3 days, taste to see if it has fermented sufficiently (this depends on climate and season). If ready, serve small dishes of the vegetables with any meal. After 5 days, you should keep the pickled cabbage in the refrigerator, where it will keep for another 7 to 10 days.

Serves 4
Preparation time: 15 mins
Pickling time: 3–5 days

Mixed Vegetable Salad
with Spicy Sweet Peanut Dressing

3 cups (250 g) spinach leaves, washed and drained, stems discarded

2¹/₂ cups (250 g) sliced green beans

4 cups (200 g) bean sprouts, tails removed, washed and drained

Deep-fried prawn crackers (see note), optional

Spicy Peanut Dressing

1 tablespoon tamarind pulp

4 tablespoons warm water

1–2 small chili peppers

1 in (2 cm) aromatic ginger (*kencur*) or galangal (see note)

4 cloves garlic

3 kaffir lime leaves, sliced

¹/₂ teaspoon dried shrimp paste, toasted

2 teaspoons salt

¹/₂ cup (90 g) shaved palm sugar or dark brown sugar

1¹/₂ cups (250 g) raw peanuts, dry-roasted, skins removed

2 cups (500 ml) hot water

Serves 4 to 6
Preparation time: 30 mins
Cooking time: 30–35 mins

1 Prepare the Spicy Peanut Dressing by soaking the tamarind pulp in the warm water for 5 minutes. Mash it with the fingers and strain to obtain the juice; set aside. Grind the peanuts coarsely in a food processor, remove and set aside. Grind the chilies, aromatic ginger, garlic, kaffir lime leaves, shrimp paste, reserved tamarind juice, salt and palm sugar to form a smooth paste. Add the ground peanuts to the spice paste and pulse a few times. Add the water and pulse to make a thick sauce.

2 Blanch or steam each type of vegetables separately for 1 to 2 minutes each, being careful not to overcook.

3 Arrange the vegetables on a plate and either spoon the Spicy Peanut Dressing over the vegetables or serve on the side in a bowl. Garnish with prawn crackers, if using, and serve at room temperature.

Aromatic ginger, also known as *kencur* or *cekor*, is sometimes called lesser galangal. This ginger-like root with a unique, camphor-like flavor should be used sparingly. Wash it and scrape off the skin before using. Dried *kencur* powder can be used as a substitute; use ¹/₂–1 teaspoon of powder for 1 in (2.5 cm) of fresh root.

Prawn crackers, or *kerupuk*, are dried wafers made from tapioca starch mixed with bits of shrimp or fish and spices, which are deep-fried until crispy then eaten as a garnish or snack. Buy them dried in plastic packets in Asian food stores. The wafers must be thoroughly dried in the oven set on low heat for 30 minutes before being deep-fried in oil for a few seconds, when they puff up spectacularly. Store fried *kerupuk* in an airtight container.

Japanese Chicken Vegetable Soup

6 cups (1.5 liters) water
10 oz (300 g) boneless chicken meat, skin removed, cut into bite-sized pieces
1 large or 2 small carrots, cut into chunks
2 cups (250 g) pumpkin, skin and seeds removed, cut into chunks
1 1/2 cups (175 g) bamboo shoots, sliced into bite-sized chunks
3 teaspoons *dashi* soup stock powder
3 tablespoons soy sauce
3 tablespoons sake
3 tablespoons mirin

1 Bring the water to a boil in a large saucepan. Add the chicken pieces and cook over medium heat for 2 minutes, removing any scum from the surface with a spoon or paper towel.
2 Add the carrot, pumpkin and bamboo shoots.
3 Stir in the *dashi* soup stock powder, soy sauce, sake and mirin. Return to a boil and cover the pan. Boil rapidly for 5 minutes, then reduce the heat and simmer covered for 20 minutes, or until the vegetables are tender.
4 Let stand for 10 minutes before serving in small bowls with a little of the cooking liquid.

Serves 4
Preparation time: 20 mins
Cooking time: 40 mins

Chinese Hot and Sour Soup

Heavily seasoned and chock-full of highly nutritious ingredients, this soup is particularly popular as a winter dish. This recipe includes various meat ingredients, but an equally tasty vegetarian version may also be prepared using vegetable stock or plain water and double the quantity of tofu and black Chinese mushrooms.

1 chicken breast
2 slices Yunnan ham or prosciutto
1 liter (4 cups) chicken stock, or plain water
2 teaspoons salt
1 teaspoon sugar
$1/2$ cup (75 g) green peas
1 cake (10 oz/300 g) firm tofu, diced
$1/2$ cup (35 g) slivered bamboo shoots
1 small carrot, thinly sliced

4 dried black Chinese mushrooms, soaked in hot water for 15 minutes then drained, stems discarded and caps diced
1 cup (15 g) sliced woodear fungus
2 eggs, well beaten
$1^1/2$ tablespoons soy sauce
2 tablespoons vinegar
2 teaspoons sesame oil
$1/2$ teaspoon ground black pepper

$1/2$ teaspoon ground Sichuan peppercorn
2 tablespoons cornstarch mixed with 4 tablespoons cool water
1 bunch fresh coriander leaves (cilantro), chopped
6 slices ginger, finely shredded
4 green onions (scallions), chopped

1 Poach the chicken and ham in boiling water for 2 minutes, then drain and set aside to cool. Shred finely with fingers or a sharp knife and set aside.

2 Bring the chicken stock or water to a boil in a large pot. Add the salt, sugar, peas and the reserved meat and vegetables and stir well. Return to a boil, reduce the heat and simmer for 3 minutes.

3 Slowly drizzle the beaten eggs across the surface of the simmering soup and leave without stirring for 1 minute.

4 Add the soy sauce, vinegar, sesame oil, black pepper and ground Sichuan peppercorn, and stir to blend for 1 minute.

5 Stir the cornstarch and water again, then pour slowly into the simmering soup while stirring gently, and keep stirring until the soup thickens. Simmer 1 more minute, then turn off the heat.

6 Serve garnished with coriander leaves, ginger and green onions.

Serves 4
Preparation time: 30 mins
Cooking time: 30 mins

Vietnamese Seafood Soup with Pineapple

While there are many versions of this popular South Vietnamese soup, the successful ones balance the sweet, hot and sour flavors that make this dish so appealing. This particular rendition, from Helene Sze McCarthy, calls for dusting the shrimp in tapioca flour or cornstarch and stir-frying them before adding them to the hot soup. This process produces a more flavorful result and gives the shrimp the added texture. This soup comes together quickly so try to have all the ingredients ready to assemble.

$1/2$ cup (60 g) cornstarch
1 lb (500 g) fresh shrimp, peeled and deveined
2 tablespoons oil
6 cups (1.5 liters) chicken stock or 2 to 3 bouillon cubes dissolved in 6 cups (1.5 liters) hot water
4 tablespoons Tamarind Juice (see note)
$1^{1}/_{2}$ cups (300 g) pineapple cubes

2 stalks celery, sliced
1 tomato, cut into wedges
8 okra, sliced
1–2 small chili peppers, deseeded and thinly sliced
2 cups (100 g) bean sprouts, tops and tails removed
2 tablespoons fish sauce
$1^{1}/_{2}$ tablespoons sugar

$1/2$ teaspoon salt
2 tablespoons Crispy Fried Shallots (see note)
Sprigs of fresh coriander leaves (cilantro), to garnish

Serves 4 to 6
Preparation time: 30 mins
Cooking time: 15 mins

1 Place the tapioca flour or cornstarch in a large bowl. Dredge the shrimp in the flour, a few at a time, until thoroughly coated. Shake off the excess flour.
2 Heat the oil in a skillet over medium heat and pan-fry the coated shrimp until pink, 1 to 2 minutes on each side. Remove from the heat and set aside.
3 Bring the chicken stock and tamarind juice to a boil over high heat in a pot. Add the pineapple and all the vegetables, mix well and return to a boil. Reduce the heat to low, stir in the fish sauce, sugar and salt, and simmer covered for about 5 minutes. Finally add the shrimp to the soup, stir well and remove from the heat.
4 Spoon the soup to individual serving bowls. Garnish with the Crispy Fried Shallots, coriander leaves and serve hot.

To make **Tamarind Juice**, mix 2 tablespoons tamarind pulp with 4 tablespoons of warm water, then mash well and strain to obtain the juice, discarding the seeds and fibers.

To make **Crispy Fried Shallots**, thinly sliced the required amount of shallots and stir-fry in oil for 2–minutes, until golden brown and crispy. Remove from the pan and drain on paper towels. Keep immediately in a sealed jar to retain crispiness.

Clear Vegetarian Tofu Soup

6 cups (1.5 liters) water
2 teaspoons salt
8–12 dried black Chinese mushrooms, soaked in hot
 water for 15 minutes and drained
2$^1/_2$ cups (150 g) fresh spinach, watercress, bok choy
 or similar greens
1 cake (10 oz/300 g) soft tofu, cubed
5 slices ginger, thinly shredded
2 sprigs fresh coriander leaves (cilantro), cut into
 short lengths

1 Bring the water to a boil over high heat in a large
pot, then add the salt.
2 Cut and discard the tough stems from the mushrooms,
then cut the caps in half (if using small caps, leave
them whole).
3 Wash and rinse the vegetables. Remove any tough
or wilted stems, and separate the leaves.
4 Add the mushrooms to the boiling water, and let
the water return to a boil, then add the tofu and ginger.
Return to a boil over medium heat, cover, and simmer
for about 20 minutes.
5 Add the vegetables and stir, return to a boil, then
simmer for 2 more minutes.
6 Serve garnished with fresh coriander leaves.

Adding a few dashes of sesame oil to this soup gives
it a rich, nutty aromatic flavor. Other popular table
condiments for this soup are freshly ground black
pepper, Sichuan Pepper-Salt Powder (page 47) and
various chili sauces. You may also use other kinds of
vegetables to make this soup. Broccoli is quite good
(but be sure to peel the stems, which are bitter), or
try cauliflower, cabbage, turnip and bean sprouts.

Serves 4
Preparation time: **20 mins**
Cooking time: **30 mins**

Light and Healthy Fish Soup with Fennel

This recipe provides a variety of therapeutic benefits, including eliminating phlegm from the body, strengthening spleen and stomach functions, and counteracting symptoms of colds and flu. Any type of white-fleshed fish may be used in this soup.

1 lb (500 g) fresh white-fleshed fish, such as sea bass or swordfish
2 tablespoons toasted sesame seeds, finely ground in a mortar or food processor (see note)
2 tablespoons oil
6 cups (1.5 liters) water or fish stock (made from bouillon cubes)
1 baby fennel bulb, halved, cored and finely sliced, leaves reserved to garnish (see note)

Seasoning
1 teaspoon soy sauce
1 teaspoon sugar
2 teaspoons fennel powder
1 teaspoon salt

Serves 4
Preparation time: **20 mins**
Marinating time: **2 hours**
Cooking time: **10 mins**

1 Rinse the fish and pat dry with paper towels, then cut into bite-sized pieces.
2 Place the ground sesame seeds in a shallow bowl, then toss the fish pieces in the sesame powder until evenly coated. Cover the bowl and allow the fish to rest in the sesame powder for about 2 hours.
3 Combine the Seasoning ingredients and set aside.
4 Heat the oil in a wok or large pot until hot and stir-fry the fish for 2 minutes, then immediately add the boiling water or fish stock. Return to a boil, then add the Seasoning and stir to mix.
5 Cover, reduce the heat, and simmer for 5 minutes. Serve garnished with fennel slices and leaves if desired.

Toast the **sesame seeds** in a frying pan over medium heat until golden brown. Keep moving the pan so the seeds do not burn.

Fennel bulbs are stumpy plants with thick stems. They have round bases that resemble large onions and have an aniseed taste. They are sold fresh in supermarkets. If fennel bulbs are not available, substitute parsley.

Tofu and Bean Sprout Soup

4 cups (1 liter) chicken or vegetable stock
1 cake (10 oz/300 g) soft tofu, cubed
1 cup (50 g) soybean sprouts (see note)
1 tablespoon preserved Chinese cabbage (tang chye—see note)
1 tablespoon fish sauce
$1/2$ teaspoon salt
$1/2$ teaspoon ground pepper
1 green onion (scallion), thinly sliced
1 sprig fresh coriander leaves (cilantro), coarsely chopped

Serves 4
Preparation time: 10 mins
Cooking time: 10 mins

1 Bring the stock to a boil in a saucepan over medium heat. Add the tofu, stirring to prevent it from sticking.
2 Add the bean sprouts when the soup returns to a boil. Cook for 2 to 3 minutes, then add the rest of the ingredients, stirring well to combine. Serve immediately.

Bean sprouts grown from mung beans are the more common variety available. **Soybean sprouts**, a larger variety, are also available in many stores. Soybean sprouts take a little longer to cook and have a nutty flavor. Always purchase sprouts fresh as they lose their crisp texture quite quickly. They will keep in the refrigerator, immersed in water, for a few days.

Tang chye is made from Chinese cabbage which is shredded and then salted and dried. It turns golden brown once preserved. It is slightly moist, with a salty flavor and crunchy texture. It is often sprinkled on rice porridge and is sometimes used to garnish noodle dishes.

Chicken and Ginseng Soup

$^1/_2$ chicken, about 1 lb
(500 g), skin and fat
removed and discarded
10 oz (300 g) lean pork
2 tablespoons sliced
ginseng (see note)
3 dried Chinese red
dates, washed and
pitted (see note)
1 slice ginger, lightly
smashed
8 cups (2 liters) water
1 teaspoon salt

Serves 2–4
Preparation time: **30 mins**
Cooking time: **2 hours**

1 Bring a pot of water to a boil. Blanch the chicken in the boiling water for 1–2 minutes, then rinse and drain. Blanch the pork the same way.
2 Place all the ingredients, except the salt, in a large pot and bring to a boil, then lower the heat and simmer for two hours. Add the salt and serve hot.

Ginseng is a highly prized medicinal root, sometimes used in cooking herbal soups. Available from Korean and Chinese supermarkets. **American ginseng** is one of the less expensive varieties of this root with a divided shape that resembles a human body. It is considered to be a general, all-healing tonic, and is available fresh or dried in supermarkets or Chinese apothecaries.

Chinese red dates, also known as *hong zao* in Mandarin, are about the size of a round olive. Although Chinese red dates are sour when raw, they are sweet when matured and dried. Red dates are often eaten during the Chinese New Year.

Chinese Red Date Soup

6 cups (1.5 liters) veg-
etable stock (made
from vegetable bouillon
cubes) or water
$^1/_2$ cup (100 g) dried
soybeans, picked
through for grit, rinsed
and soaked overnight,
then drained
2 slices ginger
1 teaspoon salt
$^1/_2$ cup (50 g) dried lily
buds washed, bases
trimmed (see note)
6 dried Chinese red
dates, washed and pit-
ted (see note, page 39)
1 tablespoon fresh
coriander leaves
(cilantro)

1 Bring the vegetable stock or water to a boil in a
large pot, then add the soybeans, ginger and salt.
Return to a boil, then cover, lower the heat and simmer
gently for 1 hour.
2 Add the lily buds and red dates. Bring the soup to a
boil again and simmer for 15 minutes.
3 Serve garnished with the coriander leaves.

Dried lily buds are the unopened buds of a variety of
Chinese day lily. The buds should be soaked and their
tough stems removed before use.

Serves 4
Preparation time: **10 mins + overnight soaking**
Cooking time: **2$^1/_4$ hours**

Corn and Tofu Chowder

1 tablespoon oil
1 teaspoon rice wine
4 cups (1 liter) vegetable or chicken stock (from fresh stock or bouillon cubes)
$1/2$ small carrot, diced
6 straw mushrooms, diced
6 fresh shiitake mushrooms, diced
1 cake (10 oz/300 g) soft tofu, diced
1 cup (200 g) fresh or frozen corn kernels
2 tablespoons green peas
1 teaspoon salt
2 tablespoons cornstarch dissolved in 2 tablespoons stock or water
$1/4$ teaspoon ground pepper
1 teaspoon sesame oil

1 Heat the oil in a wok or saucepan, then add the rice wine and let it sizzle before pouring in the chicken or vegetable stock. Bring to a boil.

2 Add the carrot and mushrooms and simmer for 5 minutes. Add the diced tofu and sweet corn, simmer another 5 minutes, then add the green peas and salt.

3 Add the cornstarch mixture and stir until the soup thickens to the consistency of chowder. Add the pepper and sesame oil and serve hot.

Serves 2–4
Preparation time: **20 mins**
Cooking time: **20 mins**

Cooling Clear Soup

This is a soothing soup with cooling, calming medicinal properties. Its Chinese name translates as "forget your troubles" and is derived from the combined effects of the tiger lily buds, bamboo pith and wolfberry, which calm "liver fire" and relax the nervous system. Chinese vegetarian cuisine has a long tradition of blending beneficial medicinal herbs with ordinary food items to create dishes that nourish the body, correct imbalances and please the palate, all at the same time.

4 cups (1 liter) vegetable or chicken stock (made from vegetable or chicken bouillon cubes)
$1/_2$ teaspoon salt
1 tablespoon dried wolfberries (see note)
$1/_2$ cup (50 g) dried lily buds, bases trimmed, soaked in water 20 minutes and drained (see note)
6 pieces fresh or dried black woodear fungus (if dried, soak in water for 20 minutes), cut into thick strips
8 pieces dried bamboo pith, soaked in cool water for 20 minutes and snipped into lengths (see note)

1 Bring the vegetable or chicken stock to a boil with the salt, then add the wolfberries, and let the water return to a boil. Add the tiger lily buds, woodear fungus and bamboo pith. Bring the soup to a boil. Cover, lower the heat and simmer for 3 minutes. Serve hot.

2 Soups like this are traditionally served with a tray of seasonings and condiments so that each person can season the soup to their own personal taste. Try the following choices: sesame oil, red chili oil, Sichuan Pepper-Salt Powder, chopped coriander leaves, chopped green onions, chopped basil leaves and chopped parsley.

Wolfberries, the fruit of the Chinese boxthorn or matrimony vine, are available dried. They look and taste a bit like small red currants but are not as sweet.

Dried bamboo pith is the dried center part of the bamboo plant. If necessary, substitute with finely cut bamboo shoot strips.

Dried lily buds are the unopened buds of a variety of Chinese day lily. The buds should be soaked and their tough stems removed before use.

Serves 4
Preparation time: 15 mins + 20 mins soaking time
Cooking time: 20 mins

Vietnamese Chicken Noodle Soup

Traditionally, this meal-in-a-bowl noodle soup is made with beef, but the Vietnamese have also perfected a lighter version using chicken. This soup is popular at any time of day or night, and is often enjoyed for breakfast in Vietnam.

10 oz (300 g) dried rice stick noodles (*kway teow* or *hofun*) or dried rice vermicelli (*beehoon* or *mifen*), soaked in water and drained

4 cups (200 g) bean sprouts, tops and tails removed, blanched

1 onion, thinly sliced

Ground pepper

1 bunch fresh coriander leaves (cilantro), sliced

1 bunch basil or coriander leaves (cilantro)

1 lime, cut into sections, to serve

2 small chili peppers, deseeded and thinly sliced, placed in a dipping bowl with soy sauce

Broth

10 cups (2.5 liters) chicken stock or 4 to 5 stock bouillon cubes dissolved in 10 cups (2.5 liters) water

1/2 fresh chicken (about 1 lb/500 g)

1 cinnamon stick

4 green onions (scallions), cut into lengths

1 in (2.5 cm) ginger, peeled and bruised

2 teaspoons sugar

1 teaspoon salt

2 tablespoons fish sauce

1 Prepare the Broth first by bringing the chicken stock, chicken, cinnamon, green onion, ginger, sugar and salt to a boil over high heat in a stockpot. Reduce the heat to low and simmer for 45 minutes, skimming off the foam and fat that float to the surface. Stir in the fish sauce and remove from the heat. Remove the chicken and set aside to cool. Strain the solids from the Broth using a fine sieve and keep the clear Broth warm over very low heat.

2 Bring a pot of water to a boil over medium heat. Add the dried noodles and blanch until soft, about 5 minutes for rice stick noodles or 2 minutes for rice vermicelli. Remove and rinse with cold water, then drain.

3 When the chicken is cool enough to handle, shred the meat along the grain into thin strips.

4 Place the noodles in individual serving bowls and top with the bean sprouts, shredded chicken and onion slices. Pour the hot Broth into each bowl, sprinkle with pepper and garnish with coriander leaves and basil leaves. Serve hot with lime and bowls of sliced chilies and soy sauce on the side.

Serves 4 to 6
Preparation time: **20 mins**
Cooking time: **1 hour**

Ramen Noodles in Clear Vegetable Broth

This dish is usually prepared with ordinary Chinese wheat noodles, dried or fresh, but any sort of noodles, such as rice noodles or dried bean thread noodles can be used as long as you follow the cooking instructions on the package labels. And, of course, you may substitute any combination of vegetables that suits your tastes and nutritional requirements.

12–16 cups (3–4 liters) water, to cook noodles
6 cups (1.5 liters) water, with 1 teaspoon salt, to make vegetable broth
8–12 dried black Chinese mushrooms, soaked in 1 cup (250 ml) hot water
8 oz (250 g) dried or 1 lb (500g) fresh Chinese wheat noodles
8 florets fresh broccoli, stems peeled, each cut into pieces
8 florets fresh cauliflower, stems peeled, each cut into pieces
1 large or 2 small heads bok choy, washed with leaves separated

Seasoning
2 green onions (scallions), minced
4 teaspoons sesame oil
2 teaspoons sugar
2 teaspoons Sichuan Pepper-Salt Powder (see note)

1 Bring the water for the noodles and the vegetable broth to a boil over high heat in separate pots.

2 Drain the mushrooms, adding the soaking water to the pot for the vegetable broth. Discard the mushroom stems and cut each cap in half.

3 Boil the noodles over high heat and cook until done, about 5 to 7 minutes for dried noodles (check the label for instructions), or about 30 seconds for fresh noodles. Drain the noodles and divide them among four serving bowls.

4 Add the mushrooms to the boiling salted water and simmer for 10 minutes. Add the broccoli and cauliflower and simmer for 2 more minutes, then add the bok choy leaves and simmer for 1 more minute. Turn off the heat.

5 Divide the Seasoning among the bowls of noodles and mix to combine.

6 With a slotted spoon or chopsticks, distribute the cooked vegetables evenly among the four bowls of noodles, then ladle enough broth from the pot to fill each bowl. Serve hot.

To make **Sichuan Pepper-Salt Powder**, dry-roast 2 tablespoons Sichuan peppercorns with $1/2$ teaspoon salt in a dry pan, then grind to a fine powder. If you cannot find Sichuan pepper, use Cajun spice mix or seasoned salt instead.

Serves 4
Preparation time: 30 mins
Cooking time: 30 mins

Vegetarian Rice Noodles

4 tablespoons oil
1 medium onion, halved and thinly sliced
5 dried black Chinese mushrooms, soaked in hot water
  for 15 minutes, stems discarded, caps thinly sliced
1 clove garlic, minced
1–2 small chili peppers, deseeded and thinly sliced
1 medium carrot, peeled and coarsely grated or sliced
1 medium green bell pepper, deseeded, cored and cut
  into thin strips
1 cake (10 oz/300 g) pressed tofu (*tau kwa*), deep-
  fried until golden brown, then cut into strips
2 cups (100 g) bean sprouts, rinsed and cleaned
2 eggs, lightly beaten
1 tablespoon soy sauce
10 oz (300 g) dried rice vermicelli (*beehoon* or *mifen*),
  soaked in hot water to soften, then drained and cut
  into 4-in (10-cm) lengths
1 green onion (scallion), cut into short lengths
Bottled or fresh chili sauce or 1–2 small chili peppers,
  sliced
2–3 small green limes, quartered, to serve

1 Heat the oil in a wok over medium heat and stir-fry
the onion until soft, about 2 minutes. Add the mushrooms, garlic and chilies, and stir-fry for 1 minute. Add
the carrot and bell pepper, increase the heat to high
and stir-fry for 2 minutes.
2 Add the *tau kwa* and bean sprouts, and stir-fry
briskly for 30 seconds. Add the egg and allow it to set a
little, about 15 seconds, then stir-fry briskly to mix
well. Add the soy sauce and stir-fry to mix well.
3 Add the *beehoon* and green onion, and stir-fry until
heated through, about 1 minute. Transfer to a serving
dish and serve with small sauce bowls of bottled or
fresh chili sauce or sliced chilies and lime on the side.

Serves 4–6
Preparation time: **20 mins**
Cooking time: **10 mins**

Tossed Spinach and Bean Threads

This is a classic Chinese *leng pan* (cold dish), in which briefly poached ingredients are tossed in a strongly seasoned sauce. A dish like this usually appears on the table first, to serve as a *kai wei* (taste opener), or appetizer or as a *jiu cai* (wine dish), or hors d'oeuvres. There are many variations of this dish, but the one given here is a tried-and-true favorite.

8 oz (250 g) fresh spinach, washed and drained
1 small bundle (3^1/$_2$ oz/ 100g) dried bean thread noodles (*tang hoon*), soaked in cool water to soften, then drained and squeezed dry by hand
2 tablespoons minced garlic

Sauce
1 tablespoon soy sauce
1 teaspoon sesame oil
^{1}/$_2$ teaspoon vinegar
1 teaspoon sugar
^{1}/$_2$ teaspoon salt
^{1}/$_2$ teaspoon ground black pepper
1 tablespoon wasabi paste

Serves 4
Preparation time: 10 mins
Cooking time: 5 mins

1 Bring a large pot of water to a boil at high heat, add the spinach and allow the water to return to a boil, about 2 minutes. Immediately remove the spinach to a colander and reserve the boiling water. Rinse under cool water and set aside to drain.
2 Mix all the Sauce ingredients in a small bowl and set aside.
3 Drop the drained bean thread noodles into the reserved boiling water. Simmer for 2 to 3 minutes, then drain and set aside (do not rinse in cool water).
4 Lightly squeeze the spinach to remove any excess water, then place on a cutting board and cut into 2-in (5-cm) pieces. Do the same with the bean thread noodles.
5 Place the spinach and bean thread noodles in a large bowl, add the garlic and the Sauce, and toss until the spinach and bean thread noodles are well mixed and completely coated with the Sauce. Transfer to a serving dish and serve.

Adding some form of seaweed enhances the flavor and the nutritional value of this dish. If the seaweed requires cooking, poach it the same way you poached the spinach and dried bean thread noodles, then cut it to a similar size. Some cooks like to garnish the finished dish with a sprinkling of minced green onions.

Chicken Soup with Bean Thread Noodles

6 cups (1.5 liters) chicken stock or 2 to 3 bouillon cubes dissolved in 6 cups (1.5 liters) hot water
1 cup (15 g) sliced woodear fungus
1 chicken breast, poached until done, then shredded
2 tablespoons fish sauce
$1/_2$ teaspoon ground black pepper
$1/_2$ teaspoon salt
4 oz (120 g) dried bean thread noodles (*tang hoon*), cut into thirds
Sprigs of coriander leaves (cilantro), to garnish

1 Bring the chicken stock and woodear fungus to a boil over high heat in a pot. Add the chicken and bring the soup to a boil again. Reduce the heat to medium and simmer uncovered for 5 to 10 minutes, seasoning with the fish sauce, black pepper and salt. Add the dried bean thread noodles, simmer for 1 to 2 minutes and remove from the heat.
2 Serve hot in individual serving bowls, garnished with coriander leaves.

You may substitute lily buds for woodear fungus, as shown in the photo. Blanch 20 dried lily buds until soft, discard the hard ends and tie each into a knot, then bring the lily buds and chicken stock to a boil in the same manner.

Serves 4
Preparation time: **10 mins**
Cooking time: **20 mins**

Fresh Tuna Rice Bowl

4 cups (400 g) freshly cooked Japanese rice
$^1/_2$ teaspoon *dashi* soup stock powder dissolved in 1$^1/_2$ cups (375 ml) water
3 tablespoons soy sauce
3 tablespoons mirin
2 teaspoons wasabi paste, or hot English mustard
1 sheet *nori* seaweed, toasted and cut in thin strips
12 oz (350 g) fresh, sashimi-grade tuna, thinly sliced
2 tablespoons Japanese pickled ginger (see note)
$^1/_2$ teaspoon sesame seeds

1 Divide the rice among 4 medium bowls.
2 Combine the *dashi* mixture, soy sauce, mirin and wasabi in a small bowl and pour over the rice. Sprinkle with the *nori*, reserving a little for decoration.
3 Arrange the tuna on top of the rice and serve topped with the reserved *nori*, pickled ginger and sesame seeds.

Japanese pickled ginger (also known as *gari*), is thinly sliced young ginger that has been pickled in sweet vinegar. Served with sushi and sashimi. Pickled older ginger (*beni shoga*), usually less sweet, is also available in jars or plastic packets from Asian food stores.

Serves 4
Preparation time: **15 mins**

Salmon Rice with Mushrooms

6 dried black Chinese mushrooms

2 cups (500 ml) boiling water

2 cups (400 g) uncooked Japanese rice

2 tablespoons soy sauce

3 tablespoons sake

3 teaspoons rice vinegar

1/2 teaspoon salt

1/2 cup (70 g) thinly sliced leek, soaked in water

7 oz (200 g) fresh salmon fillets, cleaned and skin removed

4 teaspoons mirin

2 *shiso* (or basil) leaves, thinly sliced

Nori seaweed, toasted and cut in thin strips, to garnish

Toasted sesame seeds, to garnish (see note)

Serves 4
Preparation time: 15 mins
Cooking time: 25 mins

1 Place the dried black Chinese mushrooms into a bowl, cover with 2 cups (500 ml) boiling water and soak for 15 minutes. Drain, squeezing gently to remove any excess liquid, discard the stems and slice the caps thinly. Reserve the soaking liquid to be added to the rice in Step 2.

2 Wash the rice and place in a rice cooker or large saucepan with the soy sauce, sake, rice vinegar, salt and 2 cups (500 ml) of reserved mushrooms liquid (add cold water if needed to make 500 ml). Stir to combine.

3 Place the leek, salmon and sliced mushrooms on top of the rice.

4 If using a rice cooker, cook according to the manufacturer's instructions. If not, cover the saucepan with a tight fitting lid and bring to a boil. Reduce the heat to low and simmer rice covered for 20–25 minutes or until cooked. The rice is cooked when small steam holes are visible on its surface.

5 Remove the lid, sprinkle with the mirin and gently flake the salmon with a fork. Add the *shiso* and stir lightly to combine.

6 Serve topped with the *nori* and sesame seeds.

Toast the sesame seeds in a frying pan over medium heat until golden brown. Keep moving the pan so the seeds do not burn.

Rice with Clams and Sake

2 lbs (1 kg) medium
clams in the shell or
7 oz (200 g) fresh or
canned clam meat
4 teaspoons sake
3 tablespoons soy sauce
2 teaspoons mirin
$1/_2$ tablespoon finely
shredded young ginger
5 cups (500 g) freshly
cooked Japanese rice
1 green onion (scallion),
white part only, sliced
into very fine strips

Serves 4–5
Preparation time: 30 mins
Cooking time: 10 mins

1 Scrub the clams with a brush, and soak in a large bowl of cold water for 5 minutes (if using clam meat, rinse in cold water, drain and set aside). Drain and rinse well.

2 Cook the clams covered in a medium saucepan over high heat for 3–4 minutes or until the shells open slightly, discarding any that do not open. Add a tablespoon of water if there is not enough liquid from the clams to form some steam. Drain and when cool enough to handle, remove the clam meat and discard the shells.

3 Return the clam meat (or uncooked clam meat) to the saucepan, add the sake and cook over high heat for 1 minute, stirring quickly until the meat is just cooked.

4 Add the soy sauce, mirin and ginger to the clams and continue to cook over medium heat for 1 minute. Add the clam mixture to the rice and gently fold through until combined. Serve immediately topped with green onions.

Fresh Coconut and Herb Rice Salad

1 cup (100 g) grated fresh coconut or $^3/_4$ cup (60 g) dried unsweetened coconut
$^1/_2$ cup (50 g) dried salted fish (see note)
2 tablespoons oil
3 cups (300 g) cooked rice, grains separated with a fork
1 cup (40 g) finely sliced mixed herbs (see note)
1 stalk lemongrass, tender inner part of bottom third only, thinly sliced
1 torch ginger bud (*bunga kantan*), thinly sliced (optional, see note)
5 shallots, thinly sliced
1 in (2.5 cm) young ginger, thinly sliced
$^1/_2$ in (1 cm) young galangal, peeled and thinly sliced
$^1/_2$ in (1 cm) turmeric root, peeled and thinly sliced, or $^1/_2$ teaspoon ground turmeric
$^1/_2$ teaspoon salt
$^1/_2$ teaspoon ground black pepper

Serves 4
Preparation time: **25 mins**
Cooking time: **25 mins**

1 Dry-fry the grated coconut in a wok over very low heat until golden brown, about 10 minutes for the fresh coconut and 5 to 7 minutes for the dried coconut. Set aside to cool. Then grind to a powder in a mortar or blender.

2 Rinse the dried salt fish under running water to remove excess salt, and pat dry with paper towels. Heat the oil in a skillet and cook the salt fish over medium heat until lightly browned on both sides, about 2 minutes. Set aside to cool, then tear into fine shreds.

3 Combine the rice with all the ingredients in a large bowl. Serve immediately.

Dried salted fish is used as a seasoning or condiment in Asia. Soak in water to remove excess salt before use. Squeeze dry, slice and shallow-fry until crisp.

Bunches of mixed herbs (*daun ulam*) especially for this dish are sold in Malay market stalls. These bunches include Vietnamese mint (*daun kesum* or *daun laksa*), aromatic ginger leaves (*daun cekur*), common mint (*daun pudina*), kaffir lime leaves (*daun limau purut*), young cashew leaves (*daun cajus*), wild pepper leaves (*daun kaduk*) and *ulam raja*. Any other herbs will do, including dill, celery leaves, basil, shiso, watercress, nasturtium and coriander leaves (cilantro). To shred the herbs, wash and pat dry with a clean cloth, then roll up a wad of herbs with the larger ones on the outside and slice them all very thinly with a sharp knife.

Torch ginger bud (*bunga kantan*) is the edible flower bud of the wild ginger plant. It imparts a subtle perfume to foods.

Vegetable Biryani Rice

1 cup (150 g) split mung beans or red lentils
2 tablespoons ghee or butter
1 small cinnamon stick, broken in half
6 cardamoms pods
6 cloves
3 bay leaves
2 onions, finely diced
2 in (5 cm) ginger, finely minced
1 small chili pepper, thinly sliced
$2^1/_4$ cups (450 g) uncooked long grain rice, washed
   and drained
1 teaspoon curry powder
1 cup (160 g) green peas or diced mixed vegetables
4 cups (1 liter) water
$1^1/_2$ teaspoon salt

1 Dry roast the mung beans in a wok over medium
heat for 3 to 5 minutes, or until aromatic and golden
brown. Cool thoroughly. Wash well and drain, then
set aside.
2 Heat the ghee and fry the cinnamon, cardamoms,
cloves and bay leaves over medium heat until aromatic,
1 to 2 minutes.
3 Add the onions, ginger and red chili. Stir-fry until
the onions are light brown, 2 to 3 minutes.
4 Transfer to a rice cooker. Add the rest of the ingredients and mix well. Cook according to the manufacturer's instructions. When the rice is cooked, fluff it up
with a wooden spoon. Serve with a salad or vegetable.

If a rice cooker is unavailable: Follow to Step 3. Bring
water to a boil in a deep pot. Add in all the ingredients and mix well. Reduce heat to low, cover the pot
and gently simmer, stirring occasionally until the rice
is cooked and the water, evaporated. This will take
20 to 25 minutes.

Serves 4
Preparation time: **20 mins**
Cooking time: **20 mins**

Healthy Brown Rice Congee

Millet is the oldest grain on record as a staple cereal crop in China. Although it is rarely consumed any more in the West, millet remains one of the most beneficial of all grains for human health. It is also very easy to digest and it is the only grain that alkalizes rather than acidifies the stomach. Millet lends itself best to the preparation of congee and in this recipe it is combined with the hearty flavor and chewy texture of brown rice.

1 cup (200 g) uncooked brown rice (see note)
16 cups (4 liters) water
$^1/_2$ cup (125 g) uncooked millet
1 teaspoon salt

Seasoning
1 teaspoon sesame oil
$^1/_2$ teaspoon ground black pepper
$^1/_2$ teaspoon salt
1 green onion (scallion), minced

Serves 4
Preparation time: **5 mins + 3–5 hours soaking**
Cooking time: **1$^1/_4$ hours**

1 Wash and rinse the brown rice well, then place in a large pot and add the water. Set aside to soak for 3 to 5 hours, or overnight.

2 Bring the water and rice to a boil over high heat, then add the millet and salt. When the water comes to a full boil, reduce the heat to medium-low, cover partially with a lid to allow steam to escape and simmer until it reaches the consistency of porridge, about 1$^1/_4$ hours. Stir occasionally to prevent sticking and add water as needed if it gets too dry.

3 Turn off the heat and leave the pot covered until ready to serve.

4 Mixed the Seasoning ingredients together and divide among individual serving bowls, spoon the congee on top and stir to blend the flavors.

Brown rice is rice with its golden-brown bran intact. It has more fiber than milled white rice. It also has a nutty texture.

Japanese Soba Noodles in Sweet Soy Broth

1¹/₂ tablespoons dried *wakame* seaweed (see note)

10 oz (300 g) dried *soba* noodles

4 tablespoons thinly sliced leek

2 tablespoons Japanese pickled ginger (see note)

4 eggs (optional)

¹/₄ cup (50 g) sugar, or to taste

1 cup (250 ml) mirin

5 teaspoons *dashi* soup stock powder dissolved in 4 cups (1 liter) water

¹/₂ cup (125 ml) soy sauce

Japanese seven-spice pepper powder (optional, see note)

Serves 4
Preparation time: 10 mins
Cooking time: 10 mins

1 Soak the seaweed in cold water for 5 minutes or until reconstituted. Drain and set aside.

2 Cook the noodles according to package instructions. Drain and rinse well in cold water to remove excess surface starch. Divide between 4 medium bowls.

3 Divide the reserved seaweed, leek and pickled ginger in equal portions between the 4 bowls, arrange on top of noodles and crack an egg carefully into the center of each bowl if desired.

4 Combine the sugar and mirin in a saucepan over medium heat and stir until the sugar dissolves. Add the *dashi* mixture and soy sauce, stir and bring to a boil. Pour immediately over the noodles and serve sprinkled with seven-spice pepper powder, if desired.

Wakame seaweed is sold dried in strips. Dried *wakame* is light brown and should be soaked in water before use. It is often added to soups, a few minutes before serving and has a crunchy texture. This calcium-rich seaweed may also be toasted and crumbled over soups and other dishes.

Japanese pickled ginger (also known as *gari*), is thinly sliced young ginger that has been pickled in sweet vinegar. Served with sushi and sashimi. Pickled older ginger (*beni shoga*), usually less sweet, is also available in jars or plastic packets from Asian food stores.

Japanese **seven-spice pepper powder** or *shichimi togarashi* generally includes a combination of black pepper, red chili pepper, sesame seeds, green *nori* seaweed flakes, dried orange peels, prickly ash pods and poppy seeds. It is sprinkled on noodles, one-pot meals and grilled items.

Steamed Chicken with Black Mushrooms

1 chicken, (about 2¹/₂ lbs/ 1.25 kg) cut into serving portions, or 2 lbs (1 kg) chicken pieces (breast, thigh and drumstick)
8 dried black Chinese mushrooms, soaked in hot water for 15 minutes to soften, stems removed and discarded
2 in (5 cm) fresh ginger, minced
1 tablespoon water
2 tablespoons rice wine
1 tablespoon soy sauce
1 tablespoon oyster sauce
1 teaspoon sesame oil
1 teaspoon sugar
1 teaspoon salt
1 teaspoon ground white pepper
2 tablespoons sliced green onions (scallions)

1 Put the chicken and mushrooms in a heat-proof bowl with a lid.

2 Process the ginger and water in a spice grinder, or pound the ginger in a mortar and mix with water to form a paste. Put the paste in a small sieve and press with the back of a spoon to extract the ginger juice. Sprinkle the ginger juice, rice wine, soy and oyster sauce, sesame oil, sugar, salt and pepper over the chicken and mushrooms, massaging with your hand to mix well. Stir, then cover and refrigerate for 1 hour.

3 Put the bowl inside a steamer filled with water, or place on a rack set in a deep saucepan half-filled with water. Steam over medium heat for 30–40 minutes, until the chicken is cooked, adding a little more boiling water to the steamer every 10 minutes. Transfer to a serving dish, garnish with green onions and serve hot with plain rice.

Serves 4–6
Preparation time: **15 mins + 1 hour marinating time**
Cooking time: **30–40 mins**

Chicken Rice with Ginger Chili Sauce

1 teaspoon rice wine

2 tablespoons soy sauce

1 fresh chicken (about 2$^1/_2$ lbs/1.25 kg)

2 slices fresh ginger

1 clove garlic, bruised

1 green onion (scallion), sliced

1 teaspoon sesame oil

$^1/_2$ teaspoon salt

Fresh coriander leaves (cilantro), to garnish

Freshly sliced cucumber, to garnish

Dark soy sauce or regular soy sauce, to serve

Rice

2 cups (400 g) uncooked long-grain rice

4 cups (1 liter) chicken stock to cover rice by $^3/_4$ in (2 cm)

$^1/_2$ tablespoon chicken fat (optional)

Ginger Chili Sauce

8–10 red finger-length chilies, deseeded

2 cloves garlic, peeled

$^3/_4$ in (2 cm) ginger, peeled and sliced

2 teaspoons chicken stock (from simmering chicken above)

$^1/_4$ teaspoon salt

Serves 4–6
Preparation time: **20 mins**
Cooking time: **1 hour 10 mins**

1 Combine the rice wine and 2 teaspoons of the soy sauce, and rub this mixture inside the chicken. Place the ginger, garlic and green onion inside the chicken.
2 Use a pot large enough to hold the chicken. Add enough water to cover the chicken and bring to a boil. Add the chicken, cover and turn off the heat. Allow the chicken to steep for 5 minutes. Then remove the chicken from the pot, drain the water from the stomach cavity and return the chicken to the pot. Cover and allow to steep for 25 minutes with the heat turned off.
3 Drain the chicken again and remove it from the water. Bring the water back to a boil, remove from the heat, place the chicken back in the boiling water and steep the chicken for 30 minutes. By this time, it should be cooked; leave the chicken in the water until ready to serve.
4 To make the Ginger Chili Sauce, grind all the ingredients in a mortar or blender until fine. Transfer to 4 small sauce bowls and set aside.
5 While the chicken is cooking, cook the Rice. Place the rice, chicken stock and chicken fat, if using, into a pan. Bring to a boil, then reduce the heat and simmer, covered, for 15 to 20 minutes until the rice is cooked. Alternatively, cook the rice in the stock in a rice cooker.
6 Combine the remaining soy sauce, sesame oil and salt in a small bowl. Drain the chicken and rub the soy mixture on the outside. Use a cleaver to slice the chicken, through the bones, into small serving slices. Place the chicken on a serving dish and garnish with coriander leaves and freshly sliced cucumber. Serve with small bowls of soy sauce and Ginger Chili Sauce on the side.

To make a delicious chicken vegetable broth, reserve the chicken stock and skim the fat off. Bring to a boil, add sliced cabbage, carrot, salt and pepper to taste, and garnish with freshly sliced green onions.

Soy Chicken with Vegetables

8 dried black Chinese mushrooms
1 fresh lotus root, peeled (see note)
2 tablespoons rice vinegar
1 medium carrot, peeled
1 tablespoon oil
2 boneless chicken thighs, cut into bite-sized pieces
3 tablespoons sake
1 1/2 teaspoons *dashi* soup stock powder dissolved in 1 1/4 cups (300 ml) water
2 tablespoons mirin
3 tablespoons soy sauce
12 snow peas, tops and tails removed
1 leek, shaved into strips with a vegetable peeler, to garnish (optional)

Serves 4
Preparation time: 20 mins
Cooking time: 35 mins

1 Place the mushrooms in a small bowl and add enough hot water to cover. Let stand for 15 minutes to reconstitute. Drain the mushrooms and reserve the liquid. Place the mushrooms between paper towels and squeeze gently to remove excess liquid. Cut the stems off the mushrooms.

2 Cut the lotus root in half crosswise and then slice thinly. Place in a small bowl with the vinegar and enough water to cover. Let stand for 10 minutes, then drain.

3 Cut the carrot into thin slices at an angle and set aside.

4 Heat the oil in a medium saucepan over high heat. Fry the chicken for 1–2 minutes on each side or until golden brown. Drain and discard any excess oil. Add the mushrooms, lotus root, carrot and sake. Stir well. Add the *dashi* mixture and bring to a boil removing any impurities from the surface with a spoon or paper towel. Add the mirin and half of the soy sauce. Cover and boil for 5 minutes.

5 Reduce the heat to low and simmer the mixture for another 10 minutes. Add the remaining soy sauce and snow peas and simmer, covered, for 5 minutes. Set aside for 5 minutes to cool before serving in small bowls with a little of the cooking liquid.

Lotus root has a crunchy texture and a beautiful lacy pattern when sliced crosswise. The long roots are sold fresh in Asian grocery stores, often wrapped in dried mud to keep them moist. They are also available frozen and pre-sliced in plastic packets, or canned. Fresh lotus root must be peeled before using. Substitute jicama or celery.

Steamed Chicken with Garlic Ginger Sauce

The term "exotic flavor" (*guai wei*) refers to a potent combination of spices and seasonings that combines the full spectrum of taste sensations in one harmonious blend. In addition, this blend of herbs provides a stimulating therapeutic boost to the whole system. To prepare this dish, you must first poach a whole chicken the Chinese way. This step takes about $1^1/_2$ hours (but virtually no effort) and may be done well in advance, even the day before.

1 whole chicken (2$^1/_2$ lbs/
  1.25 kgs)
1 cup (250 ml) rice wine
3 green onions (scallions),
  cut into sections
6 slices ginger
1 head iceberg lettuce
Chopped fresh coriander
  leaves (cilantro) or
  parsley, to garnish

Garlic Ginger Sauce
8 cloves garlic, minced
8 slices ginger, minced
4 green onions (scallions),
  finely sliced
1 teaspoon ground
  Sichuan peppercorn
1 teaspoon salt
1 teaspoon sugar
1 tablespoon sesame oil
1 tablespoon olive oil
$^1/_2$ teaspoon vinegar
2 tablespoons soy sauce
1 tablespoon bottled chili
  sauce (see note)
1 tablespoon sesame
  paste or tahini mixed
  with 2 tablespoons hot
  water

1 Fill a large pot two-thirds full with water, then add the rice wine, green onions and ginger slices. Bring the water to a rapid boil, then add the whole chicken, breast down. When the water returns to a boil, cover the pot tightly, reduce the heat to low and simmer for 5 minutes. Turn off the heat, wrap the pot well in several towels to keep it hot, then set the chicken aside to poach itself for about $1^1/_2$ hours. Remove it from the water and set on a rack to drain until ready to use (refrigerate if using the following day).
2 To prepare the Garlic Ginger Sauce, place the garlic, ginger and green onions in a heatproof bowl. Add the ground Sichuan peppercorn, salt and sugar. Heat the sesame and olive oils in a small skillet or wok until smoking hot, then pour over the spices in the bowl and let it sizzle. Add the vinegar, soy sauce, chili sauce and sesame paste, one at a time, stirring each well into the Sauce.
3 Cut the chicken into parts (legs, wings, breast, etc.), then either chop them into bite-sized pieces or pull the meat from the bones with your fingers.
4 Finely slice the lettuce and arrange it evenly on a large serving platter. Arrange the chicken meat neatly on top, then spoon the sauce evenly over the chicken. Garnish with fresh coriander leaves or parsley before serving.

Chili sauce is a blend of chili and water, seasoned in salt, sugar, garlic and vinegar. It is not thick and has a sweet and sour taste and is available in bottle in food stores.

Serves 4
Preparation time: **2 hours**
Assembling time: **15 mins**

Beef in Sweet Soy Broth

8 oz (250 g) beef sirloin, thinly sliced
1 tablespoon oil
2 teaspoons sake
2 teaspoons soy sauce
$1/4$ cup (30 g) leek sliced into very thin strips lengthwise and soaked in water
1 teaspoon toasted sesame seeds, to garnish (see note)

Sweet Soy Broth
2 tablespoons rice vinegar
4 teaspoons soy sauce
4 teaspoons mirin
2 tablespoons sake
2 teaspoons sugar

1 Marinate the beef in a bowl with the oil, sake and
soy sauce. Toss to combine.
2 To make the Sweet Soy Broth, combine all the
ingredients in a small pan. Heat rapidly over high
heat until the sugar dissolves. Remove from the heat
and set aside.
3 Heat a medium skillet over high heat and cook half
of the sliced beef for 1–2 minutes each side or until
cooked. Repeat with the remaining beef slices.
4 Divide the meat between 4 shallow bowls and pour
over the hot Sweet Soy Broth and let stand for
5 minutes. Garnish with the leek strips and toasted
sesame seeds. Serve warm or cold.

Toast the sesame seeds in a frying pan over medium
heat until golden brown. Keep moving the pan so the
seeds do not burn.

Serves 4
Preparation time: 15 mins
Cooking time: 10 mins

Shredded Chicken with Sesame Sauce

Often referred to in the English versions of Chinese menus as Bon Bon Chicken, presumably because it's pronounced *bang bang ji* in Chinese, this is one of the most popular chicken concoctions in Sichuan. The term *bang bang* is equivalent to the English word drumstick as a vernacular reference to the leg of the chicken. This dish is usually served as a cold appetizer at the beginning of a meal, but it may also be the main event in a simple lunch.

2 large chicken legs, about 1 lb (500 g)
$1/2$ head iceberg lettuce, or other lettuce, finely sliced
1 red bell pepper, cut in thin strips
$1/2$ teaspoon sea salt
1 teaspoon sesame oil

Sesame Sauce
$2^1/2$ tablespoons sesame paste or tahini
$1/4$ cup (60 ml) chicken stock or water
$1/2$ teaspoon ground Sichuan peppercorn
2 teaspoons sugar
1 teaspoon vinegar
1 teaspoon chili oil
2 teaspoons sesame oil
2 teaspoons dark soy sauce
$1/2$ teaspoon salt
1 tablespoon grated ginger
1 tablespoon minced garlic

1 Poach the chicken legs by placing them in a large pot with sufficient water to cover them by $1^1/4$ in (3 cm) and bring to a boil. Reduce the heat, cover tightly, and simmer for 10 minutes. Turn off the heat, and set aside to poach in the hot water for 30 minutes. Remove the chicken from the water and drain.

2 Spread the lettuce evenly on a serving plate. Place the strips of red bell pepper into a bowl with the sea salt, and mix well with your fingers to soften them. Add 1 teaspoon of sesame oil and continue to mix with your fingers until well coated, then arrange the strips evenly over the shredded lettuce.

3 Mix the Sesame Sauce by blending the sesame paste, or tahini, with the water in a bowl. Add the ground Sichuan peppercorn and mix well, then add the remaining ingredients, one at a time, stirring continuously with a whisk or fork, until well blended.

4 Remove the skin from the poached chicken and pull the meat from the bones. Tear the meat into fine shreds and pile the shredded chicken on top of the lettuce and bell peppers. Drizzle the Sesame Sauce evenly over the chicken and serve.

Serves 4
Preparation time: **20 mins**
Cooking time: **1 hour**

Pan-fried Fish Steaks Chinese-style

Red-braising is a traditional Chinese method of cooking meat, poultry and seafood. After searing the item to be cooked in hot oil, a fragrant sauce containing some sugar and soy sauce is poured over it, then the pan is covered and the food allowed to braise for a while. The characteristic dark red sheen is produced by the fusion of soy sauce, sugar and fat. Red braising is an excellent way to cook deep-water fish steaks or fillets.

1½ lbs (650 g) fresh fish steaks (tuna, halibut, seabass, swordfish or any other firm-fleshed fish), cut about ¾ in (2 cm) thick
1 teaspoon salt
¼ teaspoon ground pepper
2 green onions (scallions), cut into short lengths

Soy Ginger Sauce
2 tablespoons soy sauce
2 tablespoons rice wine
1 teaspoon sugar
1 teaspoon sesame oil
½ teaspoon vinegar
1 tablespoon grated ginger

Serves 4
Preparation time: 15 mins
Cooking time: 10 mins

1 Combine the Soy Ginger Sauce ingredients and set aside.
2 Rinse the fish and pat dry with paper towels, then sprinkle both sides with salt and pepper.
3 Heat a skillet or shallow wok over medium heat and rub the entire inside surface with a piece of fresh ginger (this helps prevent sticking). Add the oil.
4 When the oil is hot, place the steaks or fillets in the pan and fry for 2 minutes on each side. Gently shake the pan to help prevent sticking.
5 Pour the Soy Ginger Sauce over the fish. Gently shake the pan to blend and distribute the sauce evenly, then braise, uncovered, for 1 to 2 minutes.
6 Turn the fish, toss in the green onions and shake the pan. Braise for 2 more minutes and transfer to a serving dish.

For a spicier meal, add 1 tablespoon of chili paste (a blend of ground fresh or dried chilies) to the Sauce, or dust the cooked fish lightly with ground Sichuan pepper. If desired, garnish with minced coriander leaves (cilantro), which goes very well with most seafood dishes.

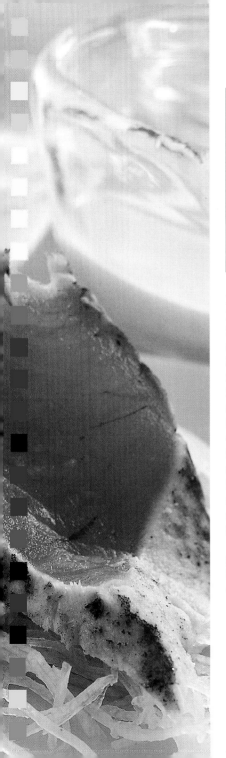

Grilled Tataki Tuna

1 lb (500 g) fresh, sashimi-grade tuna
4 teaspoons sake
4 teaspoons mirin
1 teaspoon Japanese *sansho* pepper or cracked black
  pepper
1 tablespoon oil
Shredded daikon radish, to serve

Wasabi Mayonnaise Dip
$1/4$ cup (60 ml) high-quality mayonnaise
2–3 teaspoons wasabi paste, or to taste
2 teaspoons mirin
2 teaspoons sake

1 Cut the tuna into thick strips that are approximately 1 in (2.5 cm) thick and 2 in (5 cm) wide. Marinate the fillets in the sake and mirin for 30 minutes or overnight.
2 To make the Wasabi Mayonnaise Dip, combine the mayonnaise, wasabi, mirin and sake in a bowl. Set aside.
3 Drain the marinated tuna. Combine the pepper and oil in a small baking tray and roll the drained tuna in the mixture until evenly coated.
4 Heat a pan grill or skillet over high heat and cook for 1–2 minutes on each side or until all the surfaces are sealed and the tuna is lightly browned. Remove from the pan, set aside and when cool, slice at an angle into $1/2$-in (12-mm) thick slices and arrange on a serving plate on the bed of shredded daikon radish. Serve with the Wasabi Mayonnaise Dip.

Serves 4
Preparation time: 5 mins + 30 mins marinating
Cooking time: 8 mins

Pan-fried Fish with Dill and Tomatoes

This Vietnamese fried fish sings with complementary flavors and textures, and rates high marks. This recipe will serve four as part of a larger meal, but two will finish it without any problems.

1¹/₂ lbs (700 g) fish fillets
1 tablespoon fish sauce
¹/₂ teaspoon ground black pepper
5 tablespoons flour, for dredging
4 tablespoons oil

Sauce
1 tablespoon oil
3 shallots, thinly sliced
4 cloves garlic, minced
3 ripe tomatoes, blanched, skinned and deseeded, flesh diced (or use 1 cup canned chopped tomatoes)
¹/₂ cup (125 ml) chicken stock or ¹/₄ bouillon cube dissolved in ¹/₂ cup (125 ml) hot water
1 tablespoon fish sauce
1 teaspoon sugar
1 green onion (scallion), cut into short lengths
3 tablespoons chopped dill
2 tablespoons minced coriander leaves (cilantro)
4 tablespoons chopped roasted unsalted peanuts (optional)

1 Place the fish fillets or steaks on a plate. Rub the fish sauce and black pepper into the fish, then dredge the fish in the flour until thoroughly coated. Shake off the excess flour.

2 Heat the oil in a wok or large skillet over medium heat until hot. Pan-fry the coated fish until golden brown, 4 to 5 minutes on each side. Remove from the heat and drain on paper towels. Set aside.

3 To make the Sauce, heat the oil in a wok or skillet over medium heat and stir-fry the shallots and garlic until fragrant and golden brown, 1 to 2 minutes. Add the tomatoes and stir-fry for 2 more minutes. Add the chicken stock and simmer uncovered for about 5 minutes, seasoning with the fish sauce and sugar. Finally add the fried fish, green onion, dill and coriander leaves, and mix well. Remove from the heat and transfer to a serving platter. Sprinkle the peanuts (if using) on top and serve hot with steamed rice.

Serves 4
Preparation time: 20 mins
Cooking time: 20 mins

Japanese Mixed Vegetables

1 tablespoon sesame oil
1 small onion, cut into thin wedges
1 carrot, thinly sliced
1 green bell pepper, deseeded and sliced
2 cloves garlic, minced
1 heaping teaspoon grated ginger
1 cup (80 g) snow peas, tops and tails removed
4 cups (400 g) sliced cabbage
1^1/$_2$ cups (75 g) bean sprouts, soaked in water and
    drained
2 tablespoons sake
^{1}/$_4$ teaspoon *dashi* soup stock powder dissolved in
    1 tablespoon water (substitute water or stock for the
    dashi mixture)
4 teaspoons soy sauce
1 teaspoon sugar

1 Heat the oil in a large skillet or wok over high heat
and fry the onion and carrot for 2 minutes or until
the onion is transparent. Add the bell pepper and
continue stir-frying for 2 more minutes.
2 Add the garlic, ginger and snow peas then stir-fry
for 1 minute or until fragrant.
3 Add the cabbage and bean sprouts and fry until
the cabbage starts to wilt, about 2 minutes.
4 Add the sake, *dashi* mixture, soy sauce and sugar to
the pan, stir-frying until the cooking liquid is evaporated and the vegetables are tender. Serve immediately.

Serves 4
Preparation time: 20 mins
Cooking time: 10 mins

Honey Glazed Sweet Potato Chunks

2 sweet potatoes, washed
1 tablespoon oil
4 teaspoons mirin
1 teaspoon rice vinegar
1 teaspoon soy sauce
2 teaspoons honey
1 teaspoon black sesame
  seeds, to garnish

Serves 4
Preparation time: 10 mins
Cooking time: 25 mins

1 Place the sweet potatoes in a medium pan of water. Bring to a boil, then reduce the heat to medium and cook for 15 minutes or until tender when pierced with a fork. Drain and cool.

2 Peel the potatoes thickly with a knife, removing the skin and about 2 mm of flesh. Cut into bite-sized pieces.

3 Heat the oil in a skillet over medium heat. Add the sweet potatoes and fry for 3–4 minutes or until the surface just starts to color. Add the mirin, vinegar, soy sauce and honey, then cook for 1 minute or until the liquid is reduced and starts to form a light caramel glaze around the surface of the potato. Remove from the heat, sprinkle over the sesame seeds and serve as a snack or side dish.

Soy Braised Daikon Radish

2 daikon radishes
1 teaspoon *dashi* soup
  stock powder dissolved
  in 4 cups water (or use
  any other soup stock)
2 teaspoons sugar
2 tablespoons soy sauce
4 teaspoons sake
3 tablespoons mirin

Serves 4
Preparation time: **10 mins**
Cooking time: **3 hours**

1 Remove the skin and thick outer layer and slice the daikon radish into eight thick pieces. Cut a thin strip on an angle from the top and bottom edge of each piece. Cut a shallow cross into the top on one side.

2 Place the daikon slices in a saucepan with the *dashi* mixture, sugar, soy sauce and sake. Bring to a boil, removing any impurities from the surface with a spoon. Boil for 10 minutes then reduce the heat and simmer covered for $2^1/_2$ hours or until the daikon is tender and lightly browned.

3 Gently stir in the mirin. Set aside for 10 minutes before serving in small bowls with a little of the cooking liquid.

Tofu with Ginger and Black Bean Sauce

There are probably as many ways to prepare *hong shao* (red-braised) tofu, as there are cooks in China. This traditional method of cooking tofu, which by itself is a very bland food, allows the manifold flavors of the seasoning and sauce to penetrate the tofu, rendering this potent source of vegetable protein into a delicious dish. Each time you cook this dish, try a slightly different blend of flavors and proportions until you discover the style that best suits your taste.

5–6 dried black Chinese mushrooms
1 cake (10 oz/300 g) firm tofu
3 tablespoons oil
1–2 dried red chilies, cut in half and deseeded (optional)
4–5 large cloves garlic, smashed
6 slices ginger
1 whole star anise pod (optional)
6 green onions (scallions), cut into sections

Sauce
3 tablespoons soy sauce
2 tablespoons rice wine
1 tablespoon sesame oil
1 tablespoon sugar
1 tablespoon black or yellow bean paste
$1/2$ teaspoon ground black pepper
1 teaspoon cornstarch dissolved in $1/2$ cup (125 ml) water (or use chicken stock)

1 Soak the mushrooms in warm water for about 20 minutes to soften, then drain. Remove and discard the stems, cut the caps in half and set aside.

2 Cut the tofu into bite-sized cubes. Place in a colander to drain.

3 Combine all the Sauce ingredients in a bowl and set aside.

4 Heat the oil in a wok or large skillet until hot, but not smoking. Add the chilies (if using) then the tofu, turning gently with a spatula until all the pieces are coated with oil and shaking the pan occasionally to prevent sticking. Fry until the tofu just begins to turn yellow but is not brown or crispy.

5 Add the mushrooms, garlic, ginger, star anise and half the green onions and stir-fry gently for 1 to 2 minutes.

6 Add the Sauce and stir carefully to blend. Cover the wok, lower the heat and braise for 5 to 6 minutes, adding a few tablespoons of water if the Sauce becomes too dry.

7 Add the remaining green onions to the wok and transfer to a serving dish.

Serves 4
Preparation time: 15 mins
Cooking time: 15 mins

Chinese Mixed Vegetables

1 cup (150 g) fresh or
frozen peas
2 tablespoons oil
1 1/2 cups (250 g) fresh
or frozen corn kernels
2 carrots, peeled and
diced
1 bell pepper, diced
1 onion, diced
1 cup (150 g) diced
green beans
1 in (2.5 cm) fresh
ginger, minced
1 teaspoon Sichuan
Pepper-Salt Powder
(see note)

Sauce
1 tablespoon soy sauce
1 tablespoon water
1 teaspoon sugar
1/2 teaspoon salt
1 teaspoon sesame oil

1 Remove the green peas from their pods if using fresh peas, or defrost the peas if frozen.

2 Combine the Sauce ingredients in a small bowl and set aside.

3 Heat the oil in a wok and, when hot, stir-fry the corn, carrot, bell pepper, onion, green beans, and ginger for 2 minutes.

4 Add the peas, and continue to cook for another 1 or 2 minutes.

5 Add the Sauce, reduce the heat and cook slowly for 3 to 4 minutes, then add the Sichuan Pepper-Salt Powder and stir for 1 more minute to completely blend the flavors. Serve immediately.

To make **Sichuan Pepper-Salt Powder**, dry-roast 2 tablespoons Sichuan peppercorns with 1/2 teaspoon salt in a dry pan, then grind to a fine powder. If you cannot find Sichuan pepper, use Cajun spice mix or seasoned salt instead.

Serves 4
Preparation time: **15 mins**
Cooking time: **10 mins**

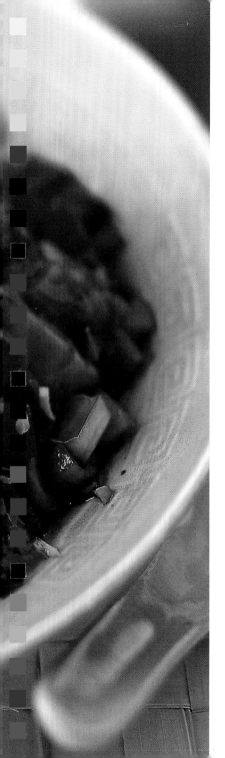

Mapo Tofu

1 cake (10 oz/300 g) soft tofu, cubed
2 tablespoons oil
2 teaspoons minced garlic
1 small chili pepper, deseeded and thinly sliced
1 tablespoon hot bean paste (see note)
2 tablespoons pickled mustard cabbage (*gai choy*), chopped (optional)
1 teaspoon wine
$^1/_4$ cup (60 ml) chicken or vegetable stock
1 tablespoon soy sauce
1 teaspoon sugar
$^1/_4$ teaspoon ground black pepper
$^1/_2$ cup (80 g) diced bell pepper
2 teaspoons cornstarch mixed with 2 tablespoons water
1 teaspoon sesame oil
1 green onion (scallion), thinly sliced, to garnish

1 Bring a small saucepan of water to a boil. Blanch the diced tofu for about 4 minutes. Rinse and drain.
2 Heat the oil in a wok and stir-fry the garlic and chili for about 1 minute. Add the broad bean paste and stir-fry until aromatic, about 1 more minute, then stir in the pickled mustard cabbage.
3 Pour in the wine, then add the chicken or vegetable stock, soy sauce, sugar and pepper, then mix to combine. Add the tofu and bell pepper, stirring carefully, then simmer over low heat for 2 minutes.
4 Add the cornstarch mixture and stir gently until the sauce thickens. Sprinkle with the sesame oil and serve hot, garnished with the chopped green onions.

Hot bean paste (*do ban jian* or *toban djan*), or chili bean sauce, is a Sichuan-style chili sauce made from chilies and fermented black beans. It is used to add heat to cooked dishes or as a dipping sauce.

Serves 2
Preparation time: **20 mins**
Cooking time: **20 mins**

Braised Tofu and Mushrooms

3 tablespoons oil
1 cake (10 oz/300 g) firm
  tofu, cut into slices
$1/4$ teaspoon salt
1 clove garlic, sliced
1 teaspoon grated ginger
10 dried black Chinese
  mushrooms, halved
  (see note)
1 carrot, sliced to yield
  about 1 cup
1 teaspoon rice wine
$1/4$ cup (60 ml) chicken
  or vegetable stock
1 teaspoon soy sauce
1 tablespoon oyster
  sauce
$1/2$ teaspoon sugar
$1/4$ teaspoon ground
  pepper
$1/2$ teaspoon cornstarch
  mixed with 2 teaspoons
  water
1 teaspoon sesame oil

1 Heat 2 tablespoons of the olive oil in a wok and fry the tofu until both sides are golden brown, 2–3 minutes on each side. Remove from the wok and drain.

2 In the same wok, heat the remaining 1 tablespoon of oil. Sprinkle in the salt and stir-fry the garlic until aromatic, about 1 minute. Stir in the grated ginger, mushrooms and carrot and stir-fry for 30 seconds.

3 Carefully add the tofu, then sizzle in the wine. Pour in the chicken or vegetable stock, soy sauce, oyster sauce, sugar, pepper and cornstarch mixture. Mix carefully, then cover and simmer over low heat for 15 minutes. Pour in the sesame oil, mix well, then serve hot.

Soak the **dried black Chinese mushrooms** in hot water for 15 minutes, then drain. Remove the stems, then slice the caps into half.

Serves 2
Preparation time: **20 mins**
Cooking time: **30 mins**

Complete Recipes Listing